A Gift For

Adrienne

From

Barbara

Date

Your Birthday

the
simple joys
of
Girlfriends
Amen

Heartwarming Stories & Inspiration to Celebrate Girlfriends

Ellie Claire
gift & paper expressions

...inspired by life

Ellie Claire® Gift & Paper Corp.
Brentwood, TN 37027
EllieClaire.com
A Worthy Publishing Company

The Simple Joys of Girlfriends
© 2013 Ellie Claire Gift & Paper Corp.

ISBN 978-1-60936-810-4

Scripture references are from the following sources: The Holy Bible, New International Version® NIV®. Copyright © 1973, 1978, 1984, 2011 by Biblica, Inc.™. Used by permission of Zondervan. All rights reserved worldwide. The Holy Bible, New King James Version (NKJV). Copyright © 1982 by Thomas Nelson, Inc. Used by permission. The New Revised Standard Version Bible (NRSV), copyright © 1989, 1995, Division of Christian Education of the National Council of the Churches of Christ in the United States of America. Used by permission. The Holy Bible, New Living Translation (NLT) copyright © 1996, 2004, 2007 by Tyndale House Foundation. Used by permission of Tyndale House Publishers Inc., Carol Stream, Illinois 60188. *The Message* (MSG) Copyright © 1993, 1994, 1995, 1996, 2000, 2001, 2002 by Eugene Peterson. Used by permission of NavPress, Colorado Springs, CO. *The Living Bible* (TLB) © 1971. Used by permission of Tyndale House Publishers, Inc., Carol Stream, Illinois 60188. All rights reserved.

Excluding Scripture verses and deity pronouns, in some quotations references to men and masculine pronouns have been replaced with gender-neutral references or feminine references.

Stock or custom editions of Ellie Claire titles may be purchased in bulk for educational, business, ministry, fundraising, or sales promotional use. For information, please e-mail info@EllieClaire.com.

Compiled by Barbara Farmer
Cover and interior design by ThinkPen | thinkpendesign.com
Illustrations by Julie Sawyer Phillips
Typesetting by Rebekah Mathis

Printed in China
1 2 3 4 5 6 7 8 9 – 18 17 16 15 14 13

Contents

I cannot count the number of times
I have been strengthened by another woman's
heartfelt hug, appreciative note, surprise
gift, or caring questions....
My friends are an oasis to me,
encouraging me to go on.
They are essential to my well-being.

DEE BRESTIN

THERE IS NO GREATER JOY

*T*ime with girlfriends is like therapy for the soul. It is the safe place where women can be "real," sharing life's burdens and celebrating daily joys. Girlfriends become salve for disappointments and amplifiers for encouragement. Girlfriend time is simply one of the best spots in any day.

Girlfriends come in all types: the tea cozy mentoring ladies, the relax on the beach girls, the hold your hand and pray through crisis sisters, the giggle through the night BFFs. Whether they are near or far, young or old, from work or the neighborhood, girlfriends add joy to life.

Our prayer is that *The Simple Joys of Girlfriends* will inspire you to celebrate all the girlfriends in your life. To embrace the gift of their friendship. To recognize every minute of girlfriend time as a beautiful gift from God.

~The Editors

CHAPTER 1

The simple joy of Old Friends

Good friends reveal themselves slowly,
in the shimmer and shadow of living...in the
years of shared experience.

*Love each other with genuine affection,
and take delight in honoring each other.*

ROMANS 12:10 NLT

New Song, Old Friend

BY BRENDA WILBEE

Clothe yourselves with love,
which binds us all together in perfect harmony.

COLOSSIANS 3:14 NLT

Last year I learned that a friend from my youth group in Arizona lived near me in the Pacific Northwest. I hadn't seen her for more than thirty-five years, and so it was an adventure to meet her again.

"Hey, you played clarinet, didn't you?" asked Rachel over coffee.

"Yes."

"You read music, right?"

"Yes."

"Want to join my church's handbell choir?"

Was she kidding?

Turns out, Rachel goes to a little church in the country, an old-fashioned one with a steeple and bell and high front steps—and a swarm of people so busy with local relief work that I get dizzy with the excitement. I drive out to this oasis every Wednesday night for a home-cooked, two-dollar supper, and hear stories of refugee support, food bank collections, and raffles for missionaries. Then a dozen of us climb creaky stairs (too steep) to the belfry (too hot), where Rachel conducts our practice, the highlight of my week.

I love the lifting of my arms, the snapping of my wrists, the clear pure note sounding in with others in perfect harmony. A friend said, "How very Currier-and-Ives of you." Perhaps, but I think the truth lies closer to the fact that my heart and soul are alive to God's work, and I am able to sing a new song with an old friend.

I breathed a song into the air;
It fell to earth, I know not where...
and the song, from beginning to end,
I found again in the heart of a friend.

HENRY WADSWORTH LONGFELLOW

Lost and Found

BY JOYCE TUDRYN FRIBERGER

*May the LORD keep watch between you and me
when we are away from each other.*

GENESIS 31:49 NIV

Winthrop, Washington, is an old western town four hours from Seattle. It was one of several stops on a summer trip my husband and I took in 1998. An unlikely tourist destination, you might say, but the mountain scenery was picture-perfect.

Eight of us met up for the Buckaroo Breakfast ride, led by a terrific teenaged guide. "Your enthusiasm reminds me of my old friend Karen," I told her. Karen and I met in the Massachusetts Junior Miss Pageant. We stayed close over the next few years through phone calls and letters, but gradually we saw each other less and less. "Along the way we lost touch," I said. I pulled out my camera. "Smile!" I wished I could send this shot to Karen, to show her how often I thought of her even after twenty years. God had given me a good friend.

We were starved when we made it to the chuck wagon. I reached for a ladle at the same time as another woman. "Are you Joyce Tudryn from Chicopee, Massachusetts?" she asked.

Karen? No way! "Look," I called to the guide. "It's my friend! The one I told you about."

"That's so awesome," the girl said. I pulled out my camera and took a picture of Karen. A good friend, who'd been hard to find.

The most beautiful discovery true friends make is that
they can grow separately without growing apart.

ELISABETH FOLEY

Someone to talk to, to laugh with,
to tell secrets to...
I'm just so thankful for the friend
I've found in you.

More Than Coincidence

BY JUDY LOGGIA

Friends love through all kinds of weather,
and families stick together in all kinds of trouble.

PROVERBS 17:17 MSG

*M*y ten-year-old, Donna, burst through the front door. "Mom, I made a new friend at school today," she said. "Can she come over tomorrow?" Donna was a shy kid, and I had been praying for her to make some friends to bring her out of her shell.

"Sure, honey, that sounds great," I said, thinking back to my own best friend growing up.

Lillian and I lived across the street from each other in Washington Heights, New York. We met at age ten too and were instantly joined at the hip. Like my daughter, I was introverted, but Lillian drew me out and boosted my confidence. She was one of the friendliest people in school. And beautiful too—with shiny black hair, so shiny it was almost indigo, and a mile-wide smile. I knew we would be best friends forever.

Senior year of high school Lillian went on a trip to Florida, the first time we'd be apart for more than a few days. "I'll be back soon," she told me. But three days later I answered my door to find Lillian's sister standing there, a pall across her face. "Judy...Lillian's..." She could hardly get the words out. My best friend had drowned on vacation.

Shortly afterward, my family moved to New Jersey. Over the years I lost touch with Lillian's family. But I still thought of her often. Tears formed in my eyes whenever I did. What I wouldn't give to feel close to her again.

The next day Donna brought her new friend home. "Hi, Mrs. Loggia," the little girl said, skipping through the front door. She flipped her hair from her shoulders—hair so shiny and black it was almost indigo—and shot me a giant smile. "My name's Lillian."

That hair. That smile. Lillian. How wonderful—my daughter's new friend was so much like the best friend I had lost.

I was still dizzy from the similarities when Lillian's mom came by to pick her up later that afternoon. I opened the door to let her in.

"Judy!" she screamed. Before I knew it, her arms had wrapped me in a tight hug. Pretty friendly for someone I had never met!

"It's me," she said, laughing. "Lillian's sister, from Washington Heights."

Yes, my daughter's friend looked familiar all right. She was my Lillian's niece. Her namesake.

A friend hears the song in my heart
and sings it to me when my memory fails.

PIONEER GIRLS LEADER'S HANDBOOK

Yes'm, old friends is always the best,
'less you can catch a new one that's fit
to make an old one out of.

SARAH ORNE JEWETT

A good friend
is a connection to life—
a tie to the past,
a road to the future,
the key to sanity in
a totally insane world.

LOIS WYSE

Rain, Rain, Go Away

BY FAYE FIELD

Two are better than one, because they have a good return for their labor:
if either of them falls down, one can help the other up.

ECCLESIASTES 4:9–10 NIV

*T*he rain came down in heavy sheets outside my window. *What a dreary day*, I thought. It was too nasty to drive to the movies or the mall; I couldn't work in the yard or sit in the garden. Nothing but gloom!

The phone rang. It was my friend Mary, whom I hadn't spoken to in a while. "I've been on a cooking spree today," she said. "I made enough stew to freeze to last a week. I baked dozens of cookies and three loaves of bread. Then I studied my Sunday school lesson. Now I'm catching up with an old friend. Don't you just love rainy days?"

By the time we hung up, my day had brightened. The rain hadn't gone away but my gloom had. I had a million things to do.

There is no friend like the old friend
who has shared our morning days,
No greeting like [her] welcome,
no homage like [her] praise;
Fame is the scentless sunflower,
with gaudy crown of gold;
But friendship is the breathing rose,
with sweets in every fold.

OLIVER WENDELL HOLMES

*Say what you want about aging,
it's still the only way to have old friends.*

ROBERT BRAULT

Writing Letters

BY PHYLLIS HOBE

*Let us consider how we may spur one another
on toward love and good deeds.*

HEBREWS 10:24 NIV

*S*ummer was gone and fall was beginning, and I decided to go through last year's Christmas cards before new ones began to arrive. I was surprised by how many I hadn't taken time to read. I put the whole pile on the dining room table, made a cup of tea, and sat down.

The first card enclosed a snapshot of two adorable kittens a dear friend had adopted after her older cat died. I remembered the joy in her voice when she called to tell me about them. Another card was from a friend who had moved to Florida when her husband retired and was enjoying the sunny weather. "When are you coming down here?" she wrote. One of the family letters went on for three pages. I savored every picture of the kids and grandkids. "What's going on in your life?" was written at the bottom of the third page, which meant why hadn't they heard from me?

There were more cards and several more letters, and when I finished them I felt as if I had spent the afternoon with loving friends. I went to my desk and began to write the first of many letters I should have written months ago.

This year I'll probably do what I always do with Christmas cards and letters: open them eagerly, glance at them quickly, and put them in a pile, because there is so little time during the holidays. But I've started a new tradition. I'll wait until life slows down again and then I'll read all the cards and letters before I answer each and every one of them with all my love.

Just a plain white homey letter came today
From a long-time friend a continent away.
Strange, I thought, that such a simple thing
Could so neatly turn a winter day to spring.

ROBERT CALDWELL

The comfort of knowing that our bond
will survive despite our differences and that
our connection provides each of us with
a more accurate picture of ourselves
enhances our chances of finding inner peace
and satisfaction as we age together.

JANE MERSKY LEDER

CHAPTER 2

The simple joy of New Friends

Friendship is like a garden of
flowers, fine and rare;
It cannot reach perfection except
through loving care;
Then, new and lovely blossoms with
each new day appear—
for Friendship, like a garden, grows
in beauty year by year.

Those who refresh others will themselves be refreshed.

PROVERBS 11:25 NLT

A Friend Found

BY INGE PERREAULT

*Behold, I send an Angel before you to keep you in the way
and to bring you into the place which I have prepared.*

EXODUS 23:20 NKJV

Riding the elevator down to the lobby after a long day at work, I found myself standing next to a handsome young man with a nice smile. A brief chat revealed what we had in common: I had only recently arrived in New York City from Germany; my companion had come from South America. We swapped stories about the difficulties of starting a new life in a new country. "I've been searching for an apartment within walking distance from my job. And what I wouldn't give for a view of Central Park!" But I was dreaming. Places like that were way out of my price range, and I hadn't found a roommate to split expenses with.

The young man wrote a number down on a scrap of paper and gave it to me. "Her name's Carole, and she's a good friend," he said. "You'll like her, and she needs a roommate."

I called her right away. "I've been waiting and waiting to hear from you," Carole said. Indeed, she became my roommate, and has been my best friend for thirty-four years.

"We were sure lucky to find each other," Carole said to me recently. "But I wondered what took you so long to call."

"What do you mean?" I said. "I called right after I ran into your South American friend."

Carole looked amazed. "Not a friend, exactly. I met him only once, and he told me about you. But that was a whole week before you finally called."

SPENDING TIME WITH A FRIEND

Relationships need time to grow. Here are some great ideas for a "girls' day out."

Share a hobby or start a new one:

Find a class to attend together like: gardening, cooking, flower arranging, pottery, home decorating, crafting, quilting, auto maintenance, jewelry making, antiquing...and the list goes on.

Take a shared hobby and start a club:

Maybe it's just the two of you or you can invite more girlfriends to join.

Chick Flick Night:

Whether it's the new release at the theater or on DVD, schedule a special night on a regular basis to enjoy a good movie together.

Meet for coffee:

As the quote says: "I am only as strong as the coffee I drink, the hairspray I use, and the friends I have."

Road Trip!:

Nothing is better than sequestered time in the car with a friend heading to a destination away from daily routines.

Pass It On Sleepover Party:

Take all the life lessons you've shared together and pass it on to the next generation. Gather your daughters and nieces and their girlfriends. Plan an overnight filled with makeovers, dance aerobics, fashion shows, and silly stories.

*Friendship isn't a big thing—
it's a million little things.*

Just Like Patsy

BY PENNEY V. SCHWAB

*We can't help but thank God for you, because your faith
is flourishing and your love for one another is growing.*

2 THESSALONIANS 1:3 NLT

My friend Patsy and I sat side by side. It was my last Sunday in the church we both loved. At dawn tomorrow our family was moving to a farm near Copeland, Kansas. I'd miss the church and our friendly Texas town. I'd miss living just down the road from my husband Don's parents. But most of all, I'd miss my friends. Especially Patsy.

Patsy shared all the bits and pieces of my life. Every Thursday evening she sat at my kitchen table and poked strained carrots down six-month-old Rebecca while I taught her oldest sons to play the piano. We shared recipes, team-taught the junior-high Sunday-school class, and took our kids for picnics when our husbands worked late. What would I do without Patsy?

She read my mind. "You'll make new friends right away," she whispered, squeezing my hand.

"Not like you," I whispered back, choking down the lump in my throat. I already knew there wouldn't be any friends like Patsy in Kansas. Everyone said so.

My mother said so: "Small towns aren't always friendly to strangers." Don's mother said so: "It will be hard to meet anyone with you living eight miles out in the country. It's a good thing the children have each other for playmates."

The children had each other. Don had the farm. But what about me? *Dear Lord*, I prayed as the pastor gave the benediction, *please give me a friend just like Patsy*.

We set out for Kansas at seven o'clock on a chilly Monday morning in February. I was certain we were heading into hostile territory. We arrived at the farm too late to begin unloading. The next day, light snowflakes turned into a snowstorm by noon and into a raging blizzard by early evening. Andi and Robert, our German shepherds, disoriented by the snow, ran away. I'd never felt so alone!

Then the telephone rang. Who could it be? No one even knew we were here. Finally I picked up the receiver. "Hello?"

"Welcome!" a friendly voice said. "I'm Audrey Button. I live in the yellow house two miles straight east. This weather is getting nasty, so I thought you might want to know who to call if you need help."

She gave me a list of numbers, then we visited for several minutes. *Maybe this is the friend I prayed for*, I thought, *the one just like Patsy*. But no. Mrs. Button's girls were grown and gone, and she and her husband were semi-retired. She was nice, but not at all like Patsy.

After two days of snow, the weather warmed up. I discovered there was something worse than being snowbound: We were now marooned by mud. That's why we were surprised when, about nine o'clock one night, there was a knock at the door. "We're Howard and Ruth Stude," a pleasant, middle-aged couple introduced themselves. They apologized for coming so late and explained they'd been afraid to try our roads before they froze semi-solid.

"We hope you'll come to our church," Ruth invited.

"We'll see," I hedged. The church she described sounded nice, but it couldn't possibly be like the one I'd left.

We went that Sunday anyway. The people were friendly and the building was lovely. There were children for ours to play with, but no babies, and no one who looked like a replacement for Patsy.

That week I went to Copeland's one small grocery store. The aisles were very narrow, and Rebecca amused herself by grabbing things from one side while I was on the other. I was afraid I'd be banned. But Annie and Edith, the proprietors, just laughed. Annie made a sign about our lost dogs and posted it in the front window. A week later the dogs were home, safe and sound.

When Patsy called to see how I was adjusting, I told her, "I've met lots of lovely people, but they're all too old, or they don't have kids the ages of mine, or we aren't interested in the same things."

"So what?" Patsy replied. "You and I aren't the same age, and we didn't have much in common when we first met. You liked sports, I liked sewing. You read mysteries, I preferred romances."

Funny, I'd forgotten all that. I'd forgotten that my friendship with Patsy had developed slowly and deepened over a period of years.

"You'll never have another friend like me," Patsy continued, "because I'm one of a kind. God only makes originals, you know. No carbon copies."

No carbon copies! In my search for a friend "just like Patsy," I'd overlooked the many "originals" God had sent my way. Friendship, I realized, wasn't a matter of age or family or common interests. It was sharing, and caring, and growing together. And it rarely came instantly. God had been answering my prayers for a friend since our first day in Copeland. He'd brought a whole community of people into my life. In time, I'd have friendships just as beautiful and deep as the one Patsy and I shared.

A Friend Like Mary

BY L. D.

If we love one another, God lives in us and
his love is made complete in us.

1 JOHN 4:12 NIV

On a recent trip, my husband and I stopped in a small beach community. As we turned onto the main street of the town, I recalled a week I'd once spent there with Mary. She was the closest friend I'd ever had. She really cared about my joys and my problems, and would encourage me to seek the Lord's will.

The memories of that time together were precious, yet painful, because a year ago Mary had died of a brain tumor. Even though I knew she was with Jesus, there was a heaviness in my heart that would not go away.

Driving home, I said wistfully to my husband, "I wonder if I'll ever have another friend like Mary."

He turned to me. "Honey," he said gently, "you can *be* a friend like Mary."

Almost immediately those words began to dissolve the ache in my heart. Instead of heaviness and pain, I felt hope. God had given me a special friend like Mary so that I could reach out and share her love with others. Our friendship did not have to end. It could touch more lives because Mary's love and caring had become a part of me.

The only way to have a friend is to be one.

RALPH WALDO EMERSON

BROWNIES IN A JAR

Use a wide-mouth quart canning jar to make this creative and delicious gift to welcome a new friend to the neighborhood, thank a friend for hosting a gathering, or just let a new friend know you are glad you met.

Ingredients

1 cup plus 2 tbsp. flour
$^2/_3$ tsp. salt
$^1/_3$ cup cocoa
$^2/_3$ cup sugar
$^2/_3$ cup brown sugar
$^1/_2$ cup chocolate chips
$^1/_2$ cup white chocolate chips
(can substitute with peanut butter or butterscotch chips)
optional: ½ cup chopped nuts or enough to fill jar to top

Directions

Combine $^1/_2$ cup plus 2 tbsp. of flour with salt and put in bottom of canning jar.

Combine cocoa and remaining $^1/_2$ cup flour and layer this brown mixture on top of the white flour and salt mixture in jar.

Layer remaining ingredients as listed. Cover with lid and colorful fabric. Secure with jar ring and tie on a tag or card with baking instructions.

Instructions for the card:
Brownies
Combine this mix with
$^2/_3$ cup oil
3 eggs, beaten
1 tsp. vanilla

Bake in an 8" square pan for 30 minutes at 350° F.

(Add a personal note like, "I hope you enjoy this special treat as much as I enjoy our friendship.")

The greatest sweetener of human life is friendship.

JOSEPH ADDISON

IN FRIENDSHIP'S GARDEN

The heart of a friend is a wondrous thing,
A gift of God most fair;
For the seed of friendship there sprouts and grows
to love and beauty rare....

Bless God for the love of friends so true,
A love akin to His,
Which knows our faults and loves us still;
That's what real friendship is.

The heart of a friend is a wondrous thing,
A gift of God most fair;
May I carefully tend the seed which grows
In friendship's garden there.

PAT LASSEN

CHAPTER 3

The simple joy of Caring Friends

Who but a good friend would put her life on hold
in order to listen, advise, sympathize, and send you on your
way secure in the knowledge that someone cares?

LOIS WYSE

Love each other as I have loved you.
Greater love has no one than this:
to lay down one's life for one's friends.

JOHN 15:12–13 NIV

Special Delivery

BY JUNE JACKSON

When God's people are in need, be ready to help them.
Always be eager to practice hospitality.

ROMANS 12:13 NLT

Around dinnertime, a friend of mine who had been recently widowed called. "The social security check hasn't arrived," she said, "and I'm out of food and money."

She lived too far away to invite her over, but at my daughter-in-law's suggestion, I called a place in her neighborhood. I explained the situation to the manager. "I'd be happy to help," he said. I tried to give him my credit card number, but he refused. "It's on us," he insisted.

Later, my friend called to thank me. "The manager brought me a big pizza," she said, "and a car full of groceries!"

That pizza parlor certainly does deliver!

In whatever [God] does in the course of our lives,
He gives us, through the experience,
some power to help others.

ELISABETH ELLIOT

*Dear friends, let us love one another,
for love comes from God. Everyone who loves
has been born of God and knows God.*

1 JOHN 4:7 NIV

Knowing what to say is not always necessary;
just the presence of a caring friend can
make a world of difference.

SHERI CURRY

WHEN A FRIEND'S IN NEED

All of you should be of one mind. Sympathize
with each other. Love each other as brothers and sisters.
Be tenderhearted, and keep a humble attitude.

1 PETER 3:8 NLT

When crisis comes to a friend or neighbor, it's often hard to know what to do or say. But at times like these, your quiet, behind-the-scenes presence can be a healing balm. Consider showing your love and concern through these suggestions:

1. Be active in prayer.

At first you may not know what to pray for, but as the situation unfolds, prayer requests will come. Start with just bringing your friend and her family to God for His comfort and peace.

2. Express love through your actions.

Help around the house is always welcome, like washing dishes, cleaning bathrooms, folding laundry, vacuuming, preparing meals, doing yard work, washing the car, shopping, taking the kids out for a breath of fresh air.

3. Be practical.

Cards and flowers are nice, but a bag or basket of everyday items such as toothpaste, toilet paper, and hand soap is even nicer. Crisis can strain a budget so gift cards for gas or groceries are always welcome. Organizing meals and/or a driving schedule can help ease your friend's stress.

4. Be positive.

Use the time you spend with your friend on positive things. Instead of lamenting over the crisis, relay uplifting stories from the neighborhood or church fellowship, or even catch up on a favorite TV show that has been missed. Help your friend go back to her routine smiling and relaxed, ready to reinvest in her situation.

5. Hold out your hand, but give her time to take it.

Offering information, suggestions, or advice can be helpful, but it can also make the person in crisis feel pushed. A simple note saying "I've been where you are, and I am available when you need me" will be an open invitation for your friend to use at her discretion.

The Gift of Friendship

BY BRIGITTE WEEKS

Your love has given me much joy and comfort...
for your kindness has often
refreshed the hearts of God's people.

PHILEMON 1:7 NLT

I don't wear a lot of makeup. But today I'm going to have brunch with my daughter and talk about her wedding next year. So, as I stood before the mirror, I reached out for a lipstick and began to put it on. As the light brown color rolled smoothly on, I realized with a sudden flash where that lipstick had come from.

Months before, as I was convalescing from a long illness, a friend had encouraged me to stop hiding and to stop feeling that I couldn't manage the routine of daily life. Her idea? "Come out to lunch," she said. "We'll go to the little restaurant across the street."

Across the street seemed to me like crossing the Red Sea. But I did as I was told, put on an outfit that had hung untouched in my closet for months, and crossed the street. My friend was already there, sitting at a comfortable table by the window looking out over the busy street, where people were going calmly about their daily lives. After we had ordered our lunch, she handed me a small gift bag. "Here," she said, "you need this."

Surprised, I looked into the bag. And there was a lipstick. Not a garish or brightly colored lipstick, but the one I am wearing today as I go with delight and eagerness to meet my daughter. After that lunch with my friend, I carefully put on the lipstick and began to look forward.

Friendship is sharing openly, laughing often, trusting always, caring deeply.

LET HER KNOW YOU CARE

Be completely humble and gentle;
be patient, bearing with one another in love.
EPHESIANS 4:2 NIV

*G*irlfriends walk the road of life side by side. When one is in a valley, the other holds her hand and supports her along the way. Some of the journeys are physical ailments, some are mental stresses, others are spiritual battles. During these times, we long to be just what our friend needs, but how can we know what's best for every situation? No matter the crisis, our outlook and perspective can help bring a positive influence. Here are some ways you can lift your friend's spirit and let her know you care.

Listen:

Sometimes words can be overrated. Sometimes we are at a loss for words. But at all times we can close our mouths and just listen. More often than not, that is what the friend in crisis needs. Listen to more than her words by taking in all that she is communicating. Her tears, her grip on your hands, her searching eyes—they all speak volumes and you can respond by touching, sharing a good cry, looking her in the eyes, and connecting.

Remind:

For a person in crisis, each day can bring a flood of negativity. Counteract it with positive reminders. Post notes of encouragement where your friend can easily find them. Sticky notes or text messages with Scripture verses of appropriate promises from God. Greeting cards or homemade posters reminding her of your love and God's love. Help her build up her strength to keep on persevering.

Share Hope:

A crisis can be a very dark place, but we have the ability to poke holes in those clouds and let rays of hope through. One way to share hope is to help your friend visualize the bigger picture. She may be in the midst of a storm, but above the stratospheric barriers the sun is shining. The weather will shift, the tide will turn, and beyond the tempest there are blue skies. And even in the midst of it, God provides sunbeams and/or umbrellas.

The only thing better than taking a moment for yourself is giving one to a friend.

Sewn Together with Kindness

BY S. M. K.

Make the most of every opportunity you have
for doing good. Don't act thoughtlessly, but try to find out
and do whatever the Lord wants you to.

EPHESIANS 5:16–17 TLB

My friend had a pile of freshly mended clothes on the front seat of her car. I noticed that a few buttons had been sewed back on with mismatched threads and the hems repaired with uneven stitches. "Who on earth did the repair work on these clothes?" I asked.

My friend smiled. "My neighbor," she answered. "She's eighty years old and lives alone."

"But you're a fantastic seamstress. You could do a much better job than this," I said.

"Oh, probably so. But my neighbor needs to be needed far more than these clothes need to be perfect."

No one is useless in this world
who lightens the burden of it for anyone else.

CHARLES DICKENS

Truly I tell you, whatever you did
for one of the least of these brothers and sisters
of mine, you did for me.

MATTHEW 25:40 NIV

If you're alone, I'll be your shadow.
If you want to cry, I'll be your shoulder.
If you want a hug, I'll be your pillow.
If you need to be happy, I'll be your smile.
But anytime you need a friend,
I'll just be me.

Just Because

BY J. M. B.

Regarding life together...you don't need me to tell you what to do. You're God-taught in these matters. Just love one another! You're already good at it; your friends...are the evidence.

1 THESSALONIANS 4:9–10 MSG

The envelope tucked among my bills, solicitations, and "occupant" flyers obviously contained a greeting card. It bore a local postmark, but what could it be? Birthday? Anniversary? Holiday? No, all were past or distant. I could think of no special event. I tore open the envelope, still wondering. Graduation? Promotion? Condolence?

Underneath a clump of blue forget-me-nots, gold lettering on the card read: "This is a Special Occasion." Inside it continued, "Another chance to say 'I Love You.'" It was signed "Maxiene." I saw her every day, but my friend had felt an extra impulse to cheer me, even though there was no special occasion.

How much better to remember a friend when there's no particular reason. Often that's when a lift is especially needed.

Hand grasps hand, eye lights eye in good friendship,
And great hearts expand,
And grow one in the sense of this world's life.

ROBERT BROWNING

The best kind of friend is the one
you could sit on a porch with,
never saying a word, and walk away
feeling like that was the best
conversation you've had.

THE GIFT OF FRIENDSHIP

A friend is a precious possession
whose value increases with years.
Someone who doesn't forsake us
when a difficult moment appears.
And our road will be smooth and untroubled
no matter what care life may send;
If we travel the pathway together,
and walk side by side with a friend.

HENRY VAN DYKE

CHAPTER 4

The simple joy of Acceptance

A friend is one who knows you as you really are,
understands where you've been, accepts who you've become,
and still gently invites you to grow.

*Therefore if you have any encouragement from
being united with Christ, if any comfort from his love,
if any common sharing in the Spirit, if any
tenderness and compassion, then make my joy complete
by being like-minded, having the same love,
being one in spirit and of one mind.*

PHILIPPIANS 2:1–2 NIV

Everyone Brings Joy

BY LINDA NEUKRUG

Clothe yourselves with compassion, kindness,
humility, gentleness and patience.

COLOSSIANS 3:12 NIV

My dear friend Helen Morrison died last year. I met her at my first job when I came to California twenty years ago. Helen never had a bad word to say about anyone. When I felt like having a good gossip about a coworker with a snappish attitude, Helen would say, "Oh, maybe he was having a bad day" in her lilting British accent. When I started to tell her about the carpool driver who leapt out of the van to chat with a friend and made me late for work, she said, "Isn't it nice to unexpectedly meet a friend?"

I once tried to get Helen to admit that a former boss we'd all found controlling and manipulative was...well, controlling and manipulative. "Come on," I coaxed, "you're not going to say you liked him!"

"Well," she said, "at times he could be a tiny bit difficult."

"A tiny bit difficult?" I exploded. "He tried to get his best friend fired! Helen, isn't there anyone you don't like?"

Helen seemed surprised by my question and considered it for several long moments. Finally she said, "When I moved to America by myself all those years ago, I knew no one. So I couldn't afford to be picky and choosy about my friends. That habit has stayed with me all these years, and it's served me well."

I must have looked skeptical because she lowered her voice and whispered in a conspiratorial tone, "Besides, Linda, everyone brings joy—some when they come and some when they go."

When we really love others, we accept them
as they are. We make our love visible
through little acts of kindness, shared activities,
words of praise and thanks.

EDWARD E. FORD

PORTABLE PARTIES

A special visit to a tearoom, a soirée, or a holiday gathering may be something that many of us enjoy with friends. However, there are those who cannot attend due to ailments or old age. Bringing the party to them will brighten up their day and yours as well.

For a tea party:
Pack up a nice serving set, pack some delicious flavored teas or plan an English tea with milk and sugar, add a fancy table linen with matching napkins and a bright bouquet of flowers. Don't forget scones or teacakes, and maybe a side of mints.

For a soirée:
Plan an afternoon or an early evening gathering for conversation or music appreciation or both. Pack a few choice hors d'oeuvres, a sparkling drink. and fancy glasses to pour it into. Don't forget a topic to discuss, or a book to read passages from, or music to listen to.

For a holiday party:

For the next upcoming holiday, bring the festivities right to your friend's door with all the appropriate garnishes and frills. Bake the pertinent dishes, plan the proper games and music, memorialize the event with photographs, and enjoy the smile on your friend's face.

A special departing gift for your friend:

When the party is over, allow your "at home guest" to sit back and relax while you clean up. More often than not, a person who is ailing or older may not have the ability to tidy up very often. Without saying a word, busy yourself with some extra cleanup beyond your own dishes and decorations.

Build Each Other Up

BY P. H. S.

Encourage each other to build each other up,
just as you are already doing.

1 THESSALONIANS 5:11 TLB

The hills of Scotland are dotted with piles of rocks called "cairns." In ancient times, it's said, a cairn symbolized both friendship and enmity. A man would begin a cairn with a small pile of rocks; then each friend who passed would add a rock while each enemy who passed would remove one.

Recently I was reminded of those cairns when I heard a friend complain that gossip was "tearing her down." I realized then that each of us can add to or take away from another's cairn of life by praise or criticism, attention or neglect, caring or contempt. Consider how our language reflects this. We speak not only of tearing someone down but also of building someone up.

Today, will you add to each life you meet, or will you take something away? Will you be a friend—or a foe? How will the cairns you pass look when you are gone? Shorter—or taller?

There is something basic about friendship.
It is like the structure that holds up a building.
It is mostly hidden and absolutely essential.

EMILIE BARNES

I entrust you to God and the message of his grace
that is able to build you up and give you an
inheritance with all those he has set apart for himself.

ACTS 20:32 NLT

To have a woman friend is to relax into another soul
and be welcomed in all that you are and all that you are not.
To know that as a woman, you are not alone.
Friendships between women provide a safe place to share
in the experiences of life *as a woman*....
It is a gift to know that you see as another sees,
an immense pleasure to be understood, to enjoy the easy
companionship of one you can let your guard down with.

STASI ELDREDGE

*Words have incredible power
to build us up emotionally.
Many of us can clearly
remember words of praise
[spoken] years ago.*

GARY SMALLEY AND JOHN TRENT

TOP TEN WAYS TO GIVE A GIRLFRIEND A "HUG"

10. Send a handwritten note to her through "snail mail."
9. Encourage her in her goals and dreams with pertinent motivational quotes.
8. Find out her favorite healthy foods and fill a basket for her.
7. Share her favorite treat so that her indulgence doesn't go to her hips.
6. Frame and give her a favorite picture of the two of you.
5. Share with her how she has made a difference in your life.
4. Spread "good gossip" about her to a mutual friend.
3. Learn her "love language" (see *The Five Languages of Love* by Gary Smalley).
2. When you're together, be all there. Your full attention is a huge encouragement.

And the number-one way to give a girlfriend a hug...
1. Give her a real hug and let her let go first.

The Ugly Truth

BY DAVE FRANCO

*Clothe yourselves...with the beauty that comes
from within, the unfading beauty of a gentle and quiet
spirit, which is so precious to God.*

1 PETER 3:4 NLT

A dear friend of ours visited us for her fortieth birthday. It had been three years since we had seen her, and she looked remarkably beautiful. All the people we introduced her to said something about her beauty, and I noticed men looking at her whenever we walked into a restaurant or a store. She had always been quite stunning, but now she seemed to be even more so. The years had not just been kind to her, they seemed to be working in her favor.

But during a long conversation, she told us that now that she was entering middle age, she couldn't believe that she was attractive anymore. Her days of feeling good about herself were over, she said, and she longed for her youth.

My first reaction was to tell her that the opposite was true. But then I realized that I could tell her that all day and I'd never truly get to the heart of the matter. What was bothering her was something much deeper than that.

And that's when it occurred to me that I was no different. I'd always felt that I had the word *failure* written on my forehead because of difficulties in my life and that it was all anybody saw when they looked at me. But if a beautiful woman like my friend could believe she was unattractive when everyone around her saw the opposite, maybe there was something wrong with my self-image too.

My friend helped me see that most of my negative thinking was based on problems that exist in only one place in the world: in my head.

A friend is someone who understands your past,
believes in your future, and accepts you
today just the way you are.

BEVERLY LAHAYE

*A friend understands
what you are trying to say...even when
your thoughts aren't fitting into words.*

ANN D. PARRISH

Friends help us feel secure.
Our footing is surer when we know that
someone accepts us as we are,
someone has our best interests at heart,
someone is always glad to see us,
someone plans to stick around. There are few
blessings like the blessing of a friend.

EMILIE BARNES AND DONNA OTTO

CHAPTER 5

The simple joy of
Keeping It Real

Friends are of utmost importance.
We love, trust, get hurt, sometimes get mad,
but we love and trust anyhow, because that's the
best way to let our friendship grow.

Trust steadily in God,
hope unswervingly, love extravagantly.
And the best of the three is love.
1 CORINTHIANS 13:13 MSG

You're Bossy

BY CAMY TANG

Do not despise the LORD's discipline, and do not resent his rebuke,
because the LORD disciplines those he loves.

PROVERBS 3:11–12 NIV

"I need to tell you something." The wary tone of my friend's voice on the phone made the feeling of dread pool in my stomach.

"What is it?" I asked.

"You said something really bossy a few weeks ago. I mentioned liking a particular store we were walking past, but you immediately said you didn't want to go inside."

At first I was defensive. "I don't even remember saying that."

"I was annoyed because I hadn't said I wanted to go inside," she continued. "I just mentioned I liked it."

I had to respect her for having the courage to tell me I had upset her. "I'm sorry I annoyed you," I said rather hopelessly.

Most of the time, I don't even realize I'm being bossy, and I don't know how to fix that part of myself. But I don't want to hurt my friends and family.

The next day I started reading the book of Proverbs, and I think God orchestrated it because He knew exactly what I needed. Verses 11 and 12 of chapter 3 reminded me to listen to this rebuke because it was not only from my friend but also from God. My friend and God love me deeply and will teach me and help me to become a better person.

A true friend is one who is concerned about
what we are becoming, who sees beyond
the present relationship, and who cares deeply
about us as a whole person.

GLORIA GAITHER

RECIPE FOR FRIENDSHIP

Ingredients:

2 heaping cups of patience
1 heart full of love
2 handfuls of generosity
1 headful of understanding
A dash of humor
Sprinkle generously with kindness
and plenty of faith

Directions:

Mix well.
Spread over a period of a lifetime.
Serve to everyone you meet.

The human contribution is the essential ingredient.
It is only in the giving of oneself to others that we truly live.

ETHEL PERCY ANDRUS

The one who loves with God's love will
not flatter, or hide anything from his friend, no
matter how difficult it may be to say....
You should be very happy if you are given
a friend who loves you in this way—
that is, a friend who wants to see you
progress in spirit and become more like Christ.
You should thank God for the day
you met a person who is like this,
for those are rare indeed.

TERESA OF AVILA

Declutter Your Mind

BY LINDA NEUKRUG

You shall...clear out the old to make way for the new.
LEVITICUS 26:10 NRSV

*D*on't put it down; put it away." A friend passed along this tip that she'd read in Dear Abby years ago. Those seven words lodged in my brain and proved very helpful in my ongoing battle against clutter. Previously, I'd find myself with a ketchup bottle in hand, for example, and think, *I'll just set it here.* An hour later I'd be looking for it and wonder why it was on my coffee table in the living room.

One day, in a grateful mood, I phoned my friend to tell her how much that saying had helped me with my goal of taming clutter. After she thanked me for letting her know, we moved on to other topics. I immediately brought up an annoying customer at work who'd come in the week before and yelled at me for not finding any books on Julia Morgan, the famous architect. "She acted like I was an idiot!" I exclaimed. My friend cut in, "Linda, remember: Don't put it down, put it away!"

"Huh?" was my inelegant response. "We're not talking about clutter here."

"Oh, but we are. That's brain clutter. Why are you still carrying around a grudge against someone, when the event happened more than a week ago?"

There was no good answer to that question, so I put it away. I found that I was happier talking about my friend's graduation from college and the customer who'd complimented me on finding just the right book for her husband's birthday.

When you stand praying,
if you hold anything against anyone,
forgive them, so that your
Father in heaven may forgive you.

MARK 11:25 NIV

A friend is a close companion on rainy days,
someone to share with through every phase...
Forgiving and helping to bring out the best,
believing the good and forgetting the rest.

Questionable Habits

BY E. GRINNAN

Everyone who competes in the games goes into strict training.
They do it to get a crown that will not last;
but we do it to get a crown that will last forever.

1 CORINTHIANS 9:25 NIV

hat would happen if you stopped exercising?" a friend teasingly asked the other day. I tried to laugh the question off, but in truth it made me feel self-conscious and a little guilty. I am a bit compulsive about getting to the gym every day.

What made me uncomfortable, I think, was the suggestion that exercise controlled me, that I was a slave to my routine and there was something selfish and self-centered about it. Couldn't some of that gym time be better spent?

That morning while I toweled off after a cycling class, I was worried enough to say a prayer: *God, if I'm too focused on this gym thing, if I've become some kind of gym rat instead of just trying to take care of the body You gave me, let me know.* It would be hard, but I could change, I told myself as I walked to work.

The first e-mail I opened was a very pleasant surprise: My friend had sent me an article about the newest findings on exercise. Well-exercised rats, apparently, are better able to handle stress and adapt to difficult situations than their sedentary rodent brethren. "Just stumbled across this," my friend's message said. "Guess it answers my question!"

And my prayer. Yet my friend's inquiry was a legitimate one. Routines can trap us sometimes, and it's always good to question them. Still, now when someone calls me a gym rat, I won't get so worried.

*There is nourishment from being encouraged
and held up by others....
We are nourished from feedback from
friends whom we trust and who
will be honest with us.*

RICH BUHLER

THE ART OF APOLOGIZING

As humans we are prone to mistakes. In relationships it is essential to apologize for said mistakes. Here are a few ideas to help you say "I'm sorry" in creative ways so that your message is loud and clear: "I value our friendship!"

Make two checklists. For the first one, write down the things that could have gone wrong and then check off the ones that did. For the second checklist, write down words that describe your feelings and check them all. Sign it, "I'm truly sorry."

Write an acrostic poem using the word "forgive" or "friend." Or use their name. Each letter of the word forms the first letter of each line of the poem.

Pack a gift basket with items that show your friend you value your relationship. A quote book on friendship, a framed picture of the two of you, a movie on friendship, a flowering plant (they last longer than bouquets), and chocolate, of course.

Write a haiku, a poem that reflects on nature and feelings describing them in a new or different way. There are three lines: five syllables in the first, seven syllables in the second, and five syllables in the third.

Take a picture of yourself slapping your forehead and make an "I'm sorry" card out of it.

Recite your own creative song, poem, or limerick over the phone or leave it on voice mail.

Go to the effort. Invest the time.
Write the letter. Make the apology. Take the trip.
Purchase the gift. Do it.
The seized opportunity renders joy.

MAX LUCADO

A Bird in the Hand

BY BRIAN DOYLE

She is clothed with strength and dignity; she can laugh at the days to come.

PROVERBS 31:25 NIV

*H*ere's the story of the day: A friend of mine who is ninety-six years old, born before the "first of the wars of the world," as she says, still lives in her little beach cottage although she's been blind since the first of our wars in "Persia," as she says. "I hear pretty well, I can move around with minimal creakiness, and people are so kind to me; why would I move?"

One morning her cat captured a sparrow outside and brought it into the house in triumph. My friend heard this dramatic adventure loud and clear while washing the dishes. She barked at the cat, picked up the fluttering bird with a sponge, opened the kitchen window, tossed out the sponge, and started back to washing the dishes, only to realize she was using the sparrow, who objected strenuously. "It was all I could do not to fall down laughing," she says, "but at my age falling down is a bad idea. I got the window open again and ejected the bird, but then I laughed so hard, I think I sprained my face."

Now, this is a terrific story from every angle imaginable, it seems to me: the deft, athletic cat; the sparrow who didn't die; the sinewy old lady giggling; the smile on your face; the prayer that your smile is for my friend; and maybe best of all, the helpless laughter of the child you will just have to tell this story to sometime today.

Through the eyes of our friends,
we learn to see ourselves...
through the love of our friends,
we learn to love ourselves...
through the caring of our friends,
we learn what it means to be
ourselves completely.

When God gives a friend, he is entrusting
us with the care of another's heart.
It is a chance to mother and to sister,
to be a Life giver, to help someone else become
the woman she was created to be, to walk
alongside her and call her deep heart forth.

JOHN AND STASI ELDREDGE

CHAPTER 6

The simple joy of
Being There

Being with you is like walking on a very clear morning—
definitely the sensation of belonging there.

E. B. WHITE

Be joyful. Grow to maturity. Encourage each other.
Live in harmony and peace.
Then the God of love and peace will be with you.

2 CORINTHIANS 13:11 NLT

Help Her Cry

BY R. H. F.

Rejoice with those who rejoice, and weep with those who weep.

ROMANS 12:15 NKJV

Half past twelve and little Wendy still hadn't come home for lunch. I called her friend's house and asked the mother to please send my daughter home. A few minutes later, Wendy came dragging dejectedly into the kitchen.

"What's wrong?" I asked. "Why didn't you come home at noon when you were supposed to?"

"Donna lost her birthday dollar," Wendy replied.

"Oh, I see. Did you stay longer to help her look for the money?"

"No, Mother, I just stayed to help her cry."

As I kissed Wendy's sweet cheek, the word "empathy" came to mind. More than "sympathy," which is looking down and pitying, empathy gets down and shares.

"I'll cry with you," she whispered,
"until we run out of tears.
Even if it's forever. We'll do it together."
There it was...a simple promise of connection.
The loving alliance of grief and hope
that blesses both our breaking apart and
our coming together again.

MOLLY FUMIA

A burden shared is a lighter load.

The greatest gift we can give one another
is rapt attention to one another's existence.

SUE ATCHLEY EBAUGH

True friendships are lasting
because true love is eternal.
A friendship in which heart speaks to
heart is a gift from God, and
no gift that comes from God
is temporary or occasional.

HENRI J. M. NOUWEN

Love one another deeply, from the heart.

1 PETER 1:22 NIV

The real key to friendship
Is a tender, gentle blend
Of this plain and simple truth—
That one must be a friend.

Friendship is based upon
What we give, not what we take,
And it steers its kindly course
For a special friend's own sake.

EDITH H. SHANK

Lord...give me the gift of faith to be renewed and
shared with others each day. Teach me to live this moment
only, looking neither to the past with regret, nor
the future with apprehension. Let love be
my aim and my life a prayer.

ROSEANN ALEXANDER-ISHAM

Simply Sit

BY CAROL KUYKENDALL

When times are good, be happy; but when times are bad, consider this:
God has made the one as well as the other.

ECCLESIASTES 7:14 NIV

What helps you most when you feel sad?" I asked a friend as we sat outside a coffee shop, enjoying the first nice day of spring and catching up with each other. Like me, she'd faced some challenges in the last year.

She fiddled with her napkin for a moment and then answered, "A friend who listens and doesn't try to rush me into 'happy.'"

I smiled at her choice of words.

"Sometimes I just need to talk about my feelings," she continued, "so I want someone to listen without trying to resolve my problem or fix me—someone who will simply sit with me in my sadness for a little while."

We fell silent for a moment and then she asked me the same question.

"What helps me most is remembering that I don't have to be afraid of feeling sad," I said. "I think of sadness as a place I go through on my way to somewhere else. It's like a dark hallway I'm passing through. And I know that God has something for me to discover in that place, so I try to explore the possibilities, like greater trust or quiet rest or the surprising way I can feel both glad and sad at the same time."

"Or that being in that place makes you a better friend to someone else who's passing through it," she added.

I remember the times you were there for me,
showing real interest and concern.
I'm thankful for the closeness we share.
How I enjoy being with you!

You keep track of all my sorrows.
You have collected all my tears in your bottle.
You have recorded each one in your book.

PSALM 56:8 NLT

Dare to love and to be a real friend. The love
you give and receive is a reality that will lead you
closer and closer to God as well as to those
whom God has given you to love.

HENRI J. M. NOUWEN

My Mystery Friend

BY EMILY IZZELL

*For the LORD comforts his people
and will have compassion on his afflicted ones.*

ISAIAH 49:13 NIV

lying has always been hard for me, so when my plane to Dallas returned to California due to a mechanical difficulty, I dreaded starting the whole trip over again. I sat at the gate, gripping my carry-on. Panic was setting in. First I'd have to get through the flight to Dallas. Then the connection home to North Carolina. *God, please help me relax.*

A woman sat beside me. "You look like you could use a friend."

"I want to get home," I told her. "But I'd give anything not to get on a plane to do it."

"You must have family waiting for you."

"My husband, Cecil. And our son." I explained I'd come out to California for a funeral. Soon we were called to another flight.

My new friend had the seat next to me. We talked more. Before catching my connecting flight I called my husband and said to expect me at midnight. My friend was next to me on that flight too. When we landed, the airport was nearly deserted. I ran to my husband and son and turned to introduce them to my companion. She was gone.

I looked for her at the baggage carousel, but she'd disappeared.

Flying is still not my favorite thing. But now I find ways to take my mind off my fear. I talk to other passengers, plan birthday presents, look at family pictures. Sometimes I think about my mysterious companion, and wonder if God sent her just for me.

*You who have received so much
love share it with others.
Love others the way that God has
loved you, with tenderness.*

MOTHER TERESA

The Cupcake Miracle

BY L. T. H.

We can't help but thank God for you, because your faith is flourishing and your love for one another is growing.

2 THESSALONIANS 1:3 NLT

Have I ever told you about the cupcake miracle?" my friend Gail asked me the other day. "It really was a sort of miracle," she went on. "I've always thought that if God spoke to anyone, it ought to be with thunder and lightning, but I guess I was wrong."

She told how she had heard that a friend was celebrating her birthday one day. There was no time to visit her friend or mail her a card, so half embarrassed by such a childlike gesture, Gail asked one of her children to put a pink candle on a grocery store cupcake and take it to her friend's home.

"I was sure she'd think I was crazy," Gail said, "but she called me the next day to say that she had been praying for a specific sign that God loved her. And when that silly little pink cupcake was delivered to her door, it seemed to her that it was a sign of God's love.

"So now I know," Gail said, "that God speaks to me in very small ways and sometimes with what seem to be just ordinary impulses. I've learned to listen," she concluded, "to God's voice in the ordinary."

*God has always used ordinary people
to carry out His extraordinary mission.*

Some blessings—like rainbows after
rain or a friend's listening ear—are extraordinary gifts
waiting to be discovered in an ordinary day.

TINA MARIE SCHUHRKE

The discovery of God lies in the daily and
the ordinary, not in the spectacular and the heroic.
If we cannot find God in the routines...
then we will not find Him at all.

RICHARD J. FOSTER

LEMON CUPCAKES WITH BLACKBERRY BUTTERCREAM ICING

These are perfect for any girlfriend get-together. Or keep them in the freezer for impromptu birthday wishes. For a gourmet touch, create an opening in the center of the cupcake and put a dollop of blackberry jam inside before icing.

Cupcakes

3 cups all-purpose flour
1 teaspoon salt
$^1/_2$ teaspoon baking powder
$^1/_2$ teaspoon baking soda
2 sticks unsalted butter, softened
2 cups sugar
$^3/_4$ cup plain yogurt
3 tablespoons lemon zest
$^2/_3$ cup lemon juice
5 eggs

1. Preheat oven to 350° F.
2. Sift together the flour, salt, baking powder, and baking soda.
3. Whisk together in a large bowl thoroughly, and set aside.
4. In a stand mixer, beat butter and sugar until smooth.
5. In a medium bowl, stir together yogurt, lemon zest, and lemon juice.
6. Add the eggs to the butter and sugar one at a time, beating in between each addition.

7. With the mixer on a low speed, add the flour mixture in 3 parts, alternating with the yogurt mixture in 2 parts. Start and end with the flour mixture.
8. Line a muffin pan with paper liners and scoop even amounts of the batter into the cups, filling almost to the top.
9. Bake for 16 minutes, rotating the pan after 8 minutes. Once golden brown around the edges, remove from oven and place on a cooling rack for at least 2 hours before icing.

Blackberry Buttercream Icing

$2^1/_2$ sticks unsalted butter, softened
1 teaspoon salt
$2^1/_2$ cups powdered sugar, sifted
$^1/_4$ cup blackberry jam (or more depending on taste)

Beat butter, 1 cup of powdered sugar, and salt until smooth. Add the blackberry jam to the mixer bowl, along with the remaining powdered sugar. Mix until fluffy and well incorporated. Place buttercream in a piping bag and pipe a circle around the outer edge of the cupcake top, spiraling in towards the center. For a fun addition, top with a fresh blackberry.

Into all our lives, in many simple, familiar, homely ways,
God infuses this element of joy from the surprises of life, which
unexpectedly brighten our days, and fill our eyes with light.

SAMUEL LONGFELLOW

When we really love others, we accept them as they are.
We make our love visible through little acts of kindness,
shared activities, words of praise and thanks, and
our willingness to get along with them.

EDWARD E. FORD

Little kindnesses, little acts of considerateness,
little appreciations, little confidences...
they are all that are needed to
keep the friendship sweet.

HUGH BLACK

CHAPTER 7

The simple joy of Admiration

If I were to make a solemn speech in praise
of you, in gratitude, in deep affection,
you would turn an alarming shade of crimson and
try to escape. So I won't. Take it all as said.

MARION C. GARRETTY

*May the Lord make your love increase and
overflow for each other and for
everyone else, just as ours does for you.*

1 THESSALONIANS 3:12 NIV

Words to Appreciate

BY ROBERTA MESSNER

Encourage one another daily, as long as it is called "Today."

HEBREWS 3:13 NIV

My sister Rebekkah and I had attended three funerals in less than a week. Each was a wonderful celebration of a life, but it bothered us that all the accolades were given *after* the person had died. "Let's tell each other what we admire about each other *now*," Rebekkah suggested.

She started. "You're the most generous person I know." A tear streamed down her cheek. "You're a great bargain hunter and, oh, what a dog lover!"

It was my turn. "You're honest, Rebekkah. And such a hard worker." I remembered the time she'd hurled herself in front of a moving truck to keep it from hitting me. "And, of course, loyal to the very end."

I was on a roll. *Why stop with my sister?* I decided. So that week, whenever I had a few minutes with a friend, I talked about my recent funeral experiences. And before I knew it, we were sharing feelings that might otherwise have gone unexpressed.

Those thank-yous felt so good that I followed them up with notes on old-fashioned stationery. I like to think of those second thank-yous being unfolded again and again on down days when a friend's heart needs the lift that, even in these days of e-mail, only handwritten correspondence can bring. They're the best buy I know of for the cost of a stamp. I should know; my sister said that I'm a great bargain hunter.

Because of a friend, life is a little stronger, fuller,
more gracious thing for the friend's existence,
whether he be near or far. If the friend is close at hand,
that is best; but if he is far away he still is there
to think of, to wonder about, to hear from,
to write to, to share life and experience with,
to serve, to honor, to admire, to love.

ARTHUR CHRISTOPHER BENSON

SIMPLE WAYS TO SAY "I LOVE YOU, GIRLFRIEND!"

1. Let your girlfriend overhear you compliment her to someone else.
2. Celebrate everyday accomplishments and simple joys, like sticking to the exercise plan or accomplishing the perfect pie crust.
3. Ask her to tell stories about her childhood and then commemorate those memories with a simple scrapbook, poem, silly song, or photo collage.
4. Remind her of something she's taught you and how much you   appreciate it.
5. Pray with her and tell God how wonderful it is having her as a friend.
6. Offer to run errands for her on days when her life is super busy.
7. Don't allow other things to distract you when your girlfriend wants to talk. Really listen. The dishes and instagram can wait.
8. Bend the rules occasionally. Saying no to desserts is great, but every once in a while share a super-sized sundae with your friend "just because."

9. Make the effort to have face time as often as possible, whether that is weekly or yearly. Use the time to let her know how thankful you are for her friendship.
10. Create a secret word, sign, or gesture of humor that only you and your girlfriend share—and use it when things are getting too serious.

Nothing, so long as I am in my senses, would I match with the joy that a friend may bring.

HORACE

The Joy of Friends

BY MARY LOU CARNEY

*What would be an adequate thanksgiving to offer God for
all the joy we experience before him because of you?*

1 THESSALONIANS 3:9 MSG

My friend Lurlene was standing in the doorway and waving when I turned down her street. By the time I'd pulled into her driveway, she was out the door and holding open her arms for a hug. "How was the trip?"

"Long," I replied. And it had been—I'd driven from my home in northern Indiana all the way to Chattanooga, Tennessee, for a visit.

We went inside, and I plopped my suitcase down in the guest bedroom. A big bouquet of orange tiger lilies—my favorite—was on the nightstand.

"Want something to eat?" Lurlene asked. "I've got fresh salsa and some crunchy cereal I know you'll like. And, oh, I found great nectarines. I know you like them better than peaches. And I picked up that movie you told me you've been wanting to see."

"You shouldn't have gone to so much trouble just for me!" I protested.

Lurlene stopped and stared at me. "Trouble? I was preparing for the arrival of my friend. That's not trouble—that's joy!"

Love is not getting, but giving....
It is goodness and honor and peace and pure living—
yes, love is that and it is the best thing in the world
and the thing that lives the longest.

HENRY VAN DYKE

The warmth of a friend's
presence brings joy to our hearts,
sunlight to our souls,
and pleasure to all of life.

TAKE TIME FOR GIRLFRIENDS

Here are ten simple things you can do together to give your relationship the attention it deserves while still having fun.

1. Walk or bike or snowshoe to the park and have lunch.
2. Have a movie marathon night with theme decorations and food.
3. Attend a music concert together dressed in your finest.
4. Plant a vegetable or flower garden and share the produce.
5. Visit all local shops together, especially the quirky ones.
6. Make a funny narration while watching videos on mute or going through photo albums.
7. Take a road trip, turn off the personal electronic devices, and really talk to each other.
8. Cook a meal together, each contributing favorite recipes.
9. Visit a nursing home or elderly person and sing songs together or offer shopping assistance.
10. Play a round of miniature golf together followed by trying on golf shoes.

I value the friend who for me finds time
on [her] calendar, but I cherish the friend who for me
does not consult the calendar.

ROBERT BRAULT

A friend is one who says, I've time,
when others have to rush.

JUNE MASTERS BACHER

*When hands reach out in
friendship, hearts are touched with joy.*

Nothing between Us

BY ISABEL WOLSELEY

The word of God is living and active...
it judges the thoughts and attitudes of the heart.

HEBREWS 4:12 NIV

I'm normally a placid, get-along-with-everybody person. Someone even told a mutual acquaintance, "You can never get into an argument with Isabel. She won't fight back." No one disagreed.

But that self-image suddenly changed one day when my best friend and I had a sharp disagreement. I told her I was right. And why I was right. And that others agreed I was right.

Later I learned that indeed I was right. It was obvious to everyone. And all those others made a point of commending me for having been right. The trouble was, I didn't feel any better about it. In fact, I felt worse.

Lord, I prayed, *You knew I was right. So why do I feel terrible now?*

I stewed about it for several days, then I finally sensed His answer: "Yes, you were right. It was your attitude that was wrong."

Instantly I knew why I had felt so uneasy, so unsettled. I might have won a little victory in a difference of opinion, but I had lost in the realm of friendship. I might have even lost a dear friend.

With that, I apologized to her. "My attitude was so wrong. Please forgive me." She did. Our warm relationship was restored.

What a relief! What difference did it really make whether I was right or wrong? I asked myself. The important part is that nothing's between my friend and me.

Friendship is the fruit gathered from the trees
planted in the rich soil of love,
and nurtured with tender care and understanding.

ALMA L. WEIXELBAUM

Let no debt remain outstanding,
except the continuing debt to love one another.

ROMANS 13:8 NIV

A BEAUTIFUL MOSAIC

No two friends are the same.
Each has his or her own gift for us.
When we expect one friend
to have all we need,
we will always be hypercritical,
never completely happy
with what he or she does have.
One friend may offer us affection,
another may stimulate our minds,
another may strengthen our souls.
The more able we are
to receive the different gifts
our friends have to give us,
the more able we will be
to offer our own unique but limited gifts.
Thus, friendships create a beautiful mosaic
of love.

HENRI J. M. NOUWEN

CHAPTER 8

The simple joy of Thankfulness

I thank God, my friend, for the blessing you are...
for the joy of your laughter...
the comfort of your prayers...
the warmth of your smile.

We always thank God for all of you
and continually mention you in our prayers.
1 THESSALONIANS 1:2 NIV

Prayer Reminders

BY DRUE DUKE

Pray about everything. Tell God what you need,
and thank him for all he has done.

PHILIPPIANS 4:6 NLT

My husband, Bob, and I celebrated our golden wedding anniversary last June. For days our mailbox was filled with beautiful cards, bringing congratulations and words of love. I saved the cards for our scrapbook and cut their colorful envelopes into small pieces to fit face down in the notepaper holder on my desk.

Now when I need to make a shopping list or jot down a telephone number, I reach for one of these pretty slips. On the reverse of the one I choose, I find the return address of a friend, and at once my heart is warmed with special thoughts. I pause a moment to speak with God about that friend.

One friend has an afflicted child; another, an aged parent. I know of two who are facing financial burdens. Then there are the happy grandparents and the man who has been promoted in his job. Each one has a special need for my prayer, be it asking for aid or voicing thanks.

From time to time all of us can use a nudge to pray for others. These little pieces of paper do the nudging for me!

LITTLE DAILY GRACES

Thank You, God, for little things
That often come our way,
The things we take for granted
But don't mention when we pray.

The unexpected courtesy,
The thoughtful kindly deed,
A hand reached out to help us
In the time of sudden need.

Oh, make us more aware, dear God,
Of little daily graces
That come to us with sweet surprise
From never-dreamed-of places.

Counting Cheerios

BY LINDA NEUKRUG

I have learned the secret of being content in any and every situation, whether well fed or hungry, whether living in plenty or in want. I can do all this through him who gives me strength.

PHILIPPIANS 4:12–13 NIV

was staying over at a friend's house and helped put her two pajama-clad boys to sleep. But first, I was touched as I listened to them say their prayers, in which they blessed everyone from Uncle Bob ("He's a soldier, you know, God.") to Twinkie, their pet yellow canary. I went to sleep with a smile, after I'd said my own prayers. *Her life seems so picture-perfect, Lord. I wish I had a beautiful house.*

The next morning, I was impressed when we sat at the kitchen table, for as soon as the boys were handed their bowls of cereal, without prompting, they bowed their heads and were silent. "Wow," I said to my friend, "they're saying grace!"

My friend burst out laughing. "They're not saying grace. They're counting Cheerios!"

"What do you mean?" I began but was interrupted by the younger boy's cry.

"*Moooom!* He got forty-four Cheerios, and I only got thirty-nine!"

That problem was quickly remedied when my friend put her hand in the box and sprinkled a few more in the bowl...and my problem of envy was quickly remedied too by a short prayer: "God, I do like her house and her boys—even her dog. But I like my own life too. Help me to remember to say thank you more often and not 'count Cheerios.'"

Gratitude unlocks the fullness of life.
It turns what we have into enough, and more.
It turns denial into acceptance,
chaos to order, confusion to clarity.
It can turn a meal into a feast, a house into a home,
a stranger into a friend.

MELODY BEATTIE

*Gratitude is the heart of contentment.
I have never met a truly thankful, appreciative
person who was not profoundly happy.*

NEIL CLARK WARREN

Little Things Mean a Lot

BY MARY ANN BOHRS

For a baby's cry,
the chirp of a bird,
the giggle of a girl,
the familiar step of a friend on the porch,
for the noise of healthy children,
Thank You, Lord.

For the fur of a kitten,
the softness of rain,
the stiffness of batter,
the plumpness of pillows,
the sure touch of my hand on another's,
Thank You, Lord.

For the incense of clean linen in the sunlight,
for cool waters on a hot day,
for the smells of a baby,
for the taste of a newly tried recipe,
Thank You, Lord.

For children's growth, before our eyes,
for seasons changing colors,
bringing hopes,
for the sight of a new friend,
and beloved familiar faces,
Thank You, Lord.

SHOW GIRLFRIEND GRATITUDE

1. Send a heartfelt, handwritten thank-you note or card.
2. Go out of your way to give her hug and say, "Thank you for all you do!"
3. Cook or bake her favorite food and drop it off to let her know how thankful you are for her.
4. Give her fresh flowers from either your garden or your floral department/shop. Tie a ribbon in her favorite color around them.
5. Take her out for coffee, tea, or lunch.
6. Offer your services: If she needs food, offer to cook a meal. If you are handy with a paintbrush, help her paint or remodel. Mow. Shop. Wash the car. Watch the dog.
7. Give her a list of all the things you are grateful for— her friendship, her prayers, her dedication, her help.
8. Reciprocate. Do for her what she has done for you. Chances are that is something she values.
9. Attend the events that are important to her. If she sings, go to her concert. If she scrapbooks, spend a day scrapping with her or helping her organize her photos.
10. Pray for her. Find out what prayer needs she has and let her know you will pray for them.

*Our prayer and God's mercy are like
two buckets in a well; while
the one ascends, the other descends.*

MARK HOPKINS

Faith is the bucket of power lowered by the rope
of prayer into the well of God's abundance.
What we bring up depends upon what we let down.
We have every encouragement to use a big bucket.

VIRGINIA WHITMAN

Gratitude reminds you of what you already have,
of gifts easily taken for granted. These can be
as small as the beauty of an almond tree in bloom
or as large as the gift of your very next breath.
When you recognize every good gift
ultimately comes from God, you can't help but
feel grateful. This deepens the pleasure
of even an ordinary day, making you not only
more content, but more generous
with what you've received.

Every good and perfect gift
is from above,
coming down from the Father
of the heavenly lights,
who does not change like
shifting shadows.

JAMES 1:17 NIV

Thank God for dirty dishes;
They have a tale to tell.
While other folks go hungry,
We're eating pretty well.

With home, and health, and happiness,
We shouldn't want to fuss;
For by this stack of evidence,
God's very good to us.

In ordinary life we hardly realize that we receive
a great deal more than we give, and that
it is only with gratitude that life becomes rich.

DIETRICH BONHOEFFER

MIGHTY MINESTRONE

A thoughtfully prepared meal can convey so many things:
"Thank you," "I'm thinking of you," "Get well soon," "Congratulations!"
Here is a shareable recipe for any occasion.

Ingredients:

3 tablespoons olive oil
1 cup chopped onion
4 cloves crushed garlic
1 cup chopped green pepper
1 cup cubed carrot
1 cup chopped celery
2 teaspoon salt
4 teaspoons Italian seasoning

$\frac{1}{4}$ teaspoon black pepper
1 medium potato, cubed
1 cup cubed or chopped zucchini
2 cans kidney and/or northern beans
5 cups vegetable stock
1 can chopped tomatoes
1 cup uncooked noodles
(ditalini or mini shells)

Directions:

- In a large kettle, sauté garlic, onions, and green pepper in olive oil until soft.
- Using 1 cup of vegetable stock, add the carrots, celery, salt, and seasonings. Bring to a boil, cover, and simmer over low heat for 10 minutes.
- Add potato, zucchini, beans in their juice, and remaining 4 cups vegetable stock. Cover and simmer 15 minutes.
- Add chopped tomatoes and their juice. Add pasta and boil gently for 10 minutes.
- Keep at low heat until you are ready to serve.
- Serves 4. Recipe is easily doubled.

THANK YOU FOR THE JOYS

I've written you in thoughts, my friend,
So often through the years,
But somehow ink just couldn't find
The words to make thoughts clear....
I've often written in my thoughts,
But here at last are words
To say I thank you for the joys
That in my heart you've stirred.

CRAIG E. SATHOFF

CHAPTER 9

The simple joy of Comfort

God bless the friend who sees my needs
and reaches out a hand,
who lifts me up, who prays for me,
and helps me understand.

AMANDA BRADLEY

Praise be to...the God of all comfort, who comforts us
in all our troubles, so that we can comfort those in any trouble
with the comfort we ourselves receive from God.

2 CORINTHIANS 1:3–4 NIV

The Comfort of Friends

BY CAROL KNAPP

There is a time for everything...
a time to weep and a time to laugh,
a time to mourn and a time to dance.

ECCLESIASTES 3:1, 4 NIV

I turned left at the four-way stop instead of continuing straight ahead toward home. I hadn't seen my eight-year-old friend Cynthia recently, and this chilly February evening seemed like a good time.

Cynthia was entertaining her best friend Hayley, whom I had never met. The girls pleaded with me to drive them to their school book fair, which was taking place that night. Being a book lover myself, I did.

We spent a wonderful time browsing through all the selections. I offered to buy them each a small item. Hayley chose a poster of cats captioned "Best Fur-riends." Then we checked out the science projects on display and ate a snack in the cafeteria.

Just one month later, Hayley died in a traffic accident. Cynthia's mother and I shared the difficult task of breaking the news to her, then drove to Hayley's house to be with her mother. There, Cynthia was asked to choose a special keepsake in remembrance of her friend. She chose the "Best Fur-riends" poster from our night at the book fair.

Who could foresee the tragedy to come when I made that sudden left at the four-way stop? I only know that God had put a desire in my heart to see Cynthia, and that gave Cynthia a last treasured night with her friend and put me in a position to comfort her.

A friend is one who joyfully sings with you
when you are on the mountain top,
and silently walks beside you through the valley.

WILLIAM A. WARD

When it's hard to look back,
and you're scared to look ahead,
you can look beside you and your
best friend will be there.

Friendship redeems.
It pulls broken parts together
and offers healing.

LUCI SHAW

Friends are an indispensable
part of a meaningful life.
They are the ones who share our burdens
and multiply our blessings.
A true friend sticks by us in our joys and
sorrows. In good times and bad,
we need friends who will pray for us, listen to us,
and lend a comforting hand
and an understanding ear when needed.

BEVERLY LAHAYE

THERE ISN'T MUCH I CAN DO

There isn't much that I can do,
but I can share my bread with you,
and I can share my joy with you,
and sometimes share a sorrow, too,
as on our way we go.

There isn't much that I can do,
but I can share my hopes with you,
and I can share my fears with you,
and sometimes shed some tears with you,
as on our way we go.

There isn't much that I can do,
but I can share my friends with you,
and I can share my life with you,
and oftentimes share a prayer with you,
as on our way we go.

The Gift of Pain

BY C. H.

Blessed are those who mourn, for they shall be comforted.

MATTHEW 5:4 NKJV

All the hardships that I thought I had faced in my life were insignificant when compared with the death, a few years ago, of a friend whom I had loved dearly and deeply. Like many people who suffer loss, I felt that God had singled me out for punishment.

Then another friend, watching me sink into self-pity, brought me a passage written by a psychiatrist for people who have lost dear ones. It read: "All your trials...are gifts to you...opportunities to grow. You will not grow if you sit in a beautiful flower garden...but you will grow if you are sick, if you are in pain, if you experience losses...and if you take the pain and learn to accept it as a gift with a specific purpose."

Pain a gift? I wondered. But then I realized that it was true. Hadn't another friend rushed to comfort me? And, in my grief, wasn't I more aware of the suffering of others? I was growing as a person. God was giving me new insights and new friends to make up for the loss I felt. And I came to know God better than ever because I needed Him to help me through my grief.

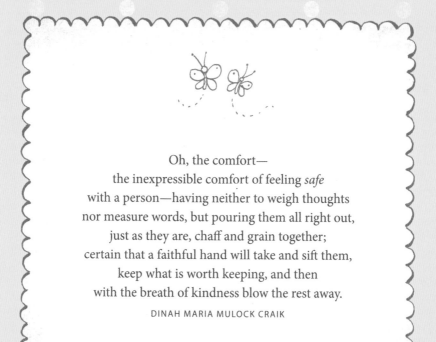

Oh, the comfort—
the inexpressible comfort of feeling *safe*
with a person—having neither to weigh thoughts
nor measure words, but pouring them all right out,
just as they are, chaff and grain together;
certain that a faithful hand will take and sift them,
keep what is worth keeping, and then
with the breath of kindness blow the rest away.

DINAH MARIA MULOCK CRAIK

Healing Laughter

BY J. MCD.

A cheerful look brings joy to the heart;
good news makes for good health.

PROVERBS 15:30 NLT

*D*uring the summer of 1967 my mother was in an automobile accident that badly cut and lacerated her face. She was stout-hearted and uncomplaining about the pain, but her temporary facial disfigurement made her self-conscious and embarrassed.

She got many cards and letters, but the one that pleased her most—and the one that restored her equanimity—was from Stanley Jones, a magazine writer and dear old friend of my family's.

Stanley wrote Mom an extravagant "love" letter in which he described elaborate plots for their elopement. He told of how he would "deck that unseemly lout with whom it is your ill fortune to be presently encumbered." (Stanley weighed barely one hundred pounds.) And he wrote florid descriptions of his tender feelings for her. Mom read it aloud to everyone who visited. It was hilarious.

How much that letter meant to my mother and father and how grateful they were to their friend, who truly understood what a gesture of sympathy is! Ever since, whenever someone dear to me is hurting, I remember Stanley Jones' thoughtful response and try to bring a little fun and laughter into my friend's life.

A good laugh is sunshine in a house.

WILLIAM MAKEPEACE THACKERAY

We can never untangle all the woes
in other people's lives.
We can't produce miracles overnight.
But we can bring a cup of
cool water to a thirsty soul, or a scoop
of laughter to a lonely heart.

BARBARA JOHNSON

How sweet the sound of friends
laughing together, of sharing the joy
of knowing each other so well.

God has not promised skies always blue,
flower-strewn pathways all our lives through;
God has not promised sun without rain,
joy without sorrow, peace without pain.
But God has promised strength for the day,
rest for the labor, light for the way,
grace for the trials, help from above,
unfailing sympathy, undying love.

ANNIE JOHNSON FLINT

How to Be a Godly Friend

BY GINA BRIDGEMAN

Use your freedom to serve one another in love; that's how freedom grows.

GALATIANS 5:13 MSG

*E*verything seemed to be going wrong for my friend Judy. Her husband had injured his back and couldn't work. Her own business had failed, and with their savings almost gone, she set out to get a full-time job—to no avail. Sinking under the stress of her situation, she became ill and was soon spending much of her time in doctors' offices.

One afternoon after a grueling round of medical tests she came over to my house and we talked. It was then that she asked the one question I was least prepared to answer: "If God really cares about me, why is He letting these terrible things happen?"

"I don't know," I feebly replied. All the Bible studies I'd attended had helped me grow in my faith, but they hadn't prepared me to help someone who was losing hers. At my next Bible study I asked my pastor and friends for advice. This is what they said:

1. *Be a caring listener.*

Sometimes the extent of Judy's anger shocked me. "I've given up on God," she told me. How was I to respond? "Show your faith by being understanding," my pastor said. Don't echo empty platitudes. Just be there. I was able to do little things, like look through the want ads with her.

2. *Take the spiritual lead.*

After several weeks of her talking and my listening, Judy said, "I feel so far from God. How can I come back?" That gave me a chance to say what I'd been thinking: Anger at God can be a part of faith. We looked at some of the many Bible passages where the main characters were tested and reacted the same way Judy did. What impressed Judy the most was that they prayed when they were angry. Anger doesn't have to keep God's people from prayer.

3. *Stay close to God.*

I never stopped praying about Judy's financial situation, her health, and her faith. It gave me the patience I needed when dealing with her directly. It also gave me the courage to ask her if she wanted to pray with me. With my encouragement she began writing down her prayers and slipping them into her Bible. Seeing even the smallest prayer answered helped restore her faith.

4. Bring your friend to church.

Judy had been away from church so long that she felt uneasy about returning on her own. "Come with me," I suggested. That Sunday I introduced her to my friends, many of whom knew about her situation and wanted to help. Sunday after Sunday Judy was able to see how much God helps us through one another. In fact, Judy and her husband eventually found new jobs through church members.

When Judy first came to me in her crisis of faith, I feared I was the last person who would know what to do. Now I think I was just the right person—not because I had any special wisdom but because I knew where to look for help. And by nurturing Judy's faith, my own faith grew as well.

Indeed, we do not really live unless we have friends surrounding us like a firm wall against the winds of the world.

CHARLES HANSON TOWNE

When we honestly ask ourselves which persons
in our lives mean the most to us, we often find it is those who,
instead of giving advice, solutions, or cures, have chosen
rather to share our pain and touch our wounds with a warm
and tender hand. The friend who can be silent
with us in a moment of despair and confusion, who can
stay with us in an hour of grief and bereavement,
who can tolerate not knowing, not curing, not healing
and face with us the reality of our powerlessness,
that is a friend who cares.

HENRI J. M. NOUWEN

CHAPTER 10

The simple joy of
God's Friendship

God's friendship is the unexpected joy we find
when we reach for His outstretched hand.

JANET L. SMITH

No longer do I call you servants, for a servant
does not know what his master is doing;
but I have called you friends, for all things that I heard
from My Father I have made known to you.

JOHN 15:15 NKJV

You've Got a Friend

God has said, "Never will I leave you; never will I forsake you."
So we say with confidence, "The Lord is my helper; I will not be afraid."

HEBREWS 13:5–6 NIV

One of the most meaningful popular songs that I've heard in recent years was written by Carole King. It is titled "You've Got a Friend." The last time I heard it, I suddenly realized why it is so popular: It promises unqualified, unlimited, unconditional friendship. If you are lonely or in trouble, the song says, "just call my name and I'll come to you." That's quite a commitment. There are few people in life upon whom we can count to help us whenever we have needs.

If you are fortunate, you may have a handful of family members and friends who would help in any adversity. As we get older that list may dwindle, but the Bible tells us that we all have at least one friend available—always. That's Jesus. If you have a problem today that is too big to handle and you feel alone, call on Him in Heaven. You've got a Friend.

God wants you to know Him
as personally as He knows you.
He craves a genuine relationship with you.
What does that look like?
In many ways, it takes the same effort other
relationships take. People don't become best friends
without talking to each other, without
spending time together, without getting to know
each other. You can't grow closer without
investing in the relationship.
That's how it works with God too.

TOM RICHARDS

*Look deep within yourself and recognize
what brings life and grace into your heart. It is this
that can be shared with those around you.
You are loved by God. This is an inspiration to love.*

CHRISTOPHER DE VINCK

Friendship with God is a two-way street....
Close friends communicate thoroughly and make
a transfer of heart and thought.
How awesome is our opportunity to be friends
with God, the almighty Creator of all!

BEVERLY LAHAYE

The very possibility of friendship with God
transfigures life. This conviction...
tends inevitably to deepen every human friendship,
to make it vastly more significant.

HENRY CHURCHILL KING

I'm asking God for one thing,
only one thing:
To live with him in his house
my whole life long.
I'll contemplate his beauty;
I'll study at his feet.
That's the only quiet, secure place
in a noisy world,
The perfect getaway.

PSALM 27:4–5 MSG

God, Our Refuge

BY HELEN GRACE LESCHEID

God is our refuge and strength, a very present help in trouble.

PSALM 46:1 NKJV

*T*rouble had come at me from all sides, and I wondered how much more I could take. I needed help, so I went to see an elderly friend whose counsel I respected. "My husband's not getting any better," I began. "Every time I see him, he's worse."

My friend nodded. He'd seen my husband in the high-security ward at Riverview, British Columbia's provincial mental hospital. After three years of aggressive treatment, there was still no sign of improvement. Besides, other stresses had bombarded our family of seven: I had totaled our car; an explosion had sent our thirteen-year-old son to the hospital; my daughter was leaving home for Europe; and illness had made me miss too many days at work, jeopardizing my nursing job.

My friend listened to my outpouring without interruption. Then he asked, "Helen, does God still love you?"

Stunned, I looked at his kind face. I wasn't prepared for this simple question. "Yes," I stammered. "Yes, I think so. The Bible says God's love is everlasting, so it's got to be the same whether my life is good or bad, doesn't it?"

He nodded. "You can stand on this fact: God loves you and will never leave you. Knowing that, you will cope." Then he smiled and said, "Now, before you go home, let's pray."

"Father," he prayed, "I thank You for my sister here. Thank You for Your great love for her. Thank You that You're with her now and always will be. Amen."

During the drive home, I reflected on our visit. My friend hadn't really answered my questions; he hadn't said very much. All he'd done was remind me that I have a refuge. And isn't that what a person lost in a raging storm needs most in life?

Be. Just be. Don't think. Don't do.
Just be. Let God fill you with His peace,
His love, His plans for you.
He will surprise you if you let Him.

Thank You for the world so sweet,
Thank You for the food we eat,
Thank You for the birds that sing,
Thank You, God, for everything.
Amen.

THE LORD'S PRAYER

Our Father who is in heaven, hallowed be Your name.
Your kingdom come. Your will be done, on earth as it is in heaven.
Give us this day our daily bread.
And forgive us our debts, as we also have forgiven our debtors.
And do not lead us into temptation, but deliver us from evil.
For Yours is the kingdom and the power and the glory forever. Amen.

MATTHEW 6:9–13 NIV

RELAXING TEA BLEND

Make this blend of tea to have on hand when you want to relax.
It is great to sip while having devotions or before prayer time.

1 tablespoon chamomile
1 tablespoon spearmint
1 tablespoon catmint
1 tablespoon rose petals
1 tablespoon green tea
2 teaspoons of rosehips

Mix all ingredients and store in an airtight container.

To make tea, add 1 teaspoon of tea blend to 1 cup almost boiling water. Cover and let sit for 5 minutes.

You're Invited

BY B. R. G.

God hasn't invited us into a disorderly, unkempt life but into something
holy and beautiful—as beautiful on the inside as the outside.

1 THESSALONIANS 4:7 MSG

Not long ago I had an unexpected invitation from a new friend at work. I knew she had a cottage at the shore. Dot's note, deposited on my desk, said simply, "If you're free the weekend after next, I'd like you to join me in Chincoteague."

I was free. "But who's going?" I asked another friend. "What's the occasion, I wonder?"

"Stop fretting," she said. "The main thing is, you're wanted!"

So I wrote a note and told Dot, "Yes, I'll come with pleasure!"

Jesus sends us a loving invitation too. We don't need to know why He has chosen us. We don't need a list of questions before we decide to accept. He simply says, "I want you. Will you come?"

Are you tired? Worn out? Burned out on religion?
Come to me. Get away with me and you'll recover your life.
I'll show you how to take a real rest.
Walk with me and work with me—watch how I do it.
Learn the unforced rhythms of grace.
I won't lay anything heavy or ill-fitting on you. .
Keep company with me and you'll learn
to live freely and lightly.

MATTHEW 11:28–30 MSG

After the friendship of God,
a friend's affection is the greatest
treasure here below.

ACKNOWLEDGMENTS